ISHTAR AND TAMMUZ: A BABYLONIAN SEASONAL MYTH

GOLU KUMAR

Contents

ONE

Forms of Tammuz, The Weeping Ceremony, Tammuz the Patriarch and the Dying God, The Mediterranean Racial Myth, Animal Forms of Gods of Fertility, Two Legends of Tammuz's Death, Attis, Adonis, and Diarmid Slain by a Boar, Laments for Tammuz, His Soul in the Underworld and the Deep, Myth of the Child God of Ocean, Sargon Myth, and Other

Versions include The Germanic Scyld of the Sheaf; Tammuz Links with Frey, Heimdal, Agni, &c.; The Assyrian Legend of "Descent of Ishtar"; The Sumerian Version; The Egyptian Isis and Nephthys; The Goddesses as Mothers, Sisters, and Wives; The Great Mothers of Babylonia; The Goddess with Seven Periods of Youth; The Lovers of Germanic

Among the gods of Babylonia, none achieved wider and more enduring fame than Tammuz, who was loved by Ishtar, the amorous Queen of Heaven--the beautiful youth who died and was mourned for and came to life again. He does not figure by his popular name in any of the city pantheons, but from the earliest times which we know about the passing of Babylonian civilization, he played a prominent part in the religious life of the people.

Tammuz, like Osiris of Egypt, was an agricultural deity, and as the Babylonian harvest was the gift of the rivers, one of his several forms was probably Dumu-Zi-Abzu, "Tammuz of the Abyss". He was also "the child", "the heroic lord", "the sentinel", "the healer", and the patriarch who reigned over the early Babylonians for a considerable period. "Tammuz of the Abyss" was one of the members of the family of Ea, god of the Deep, whose other sons, in addition to Merodach, were Nira, an obscure deity; Ki-Gulla, "world destroyer", Burnunta-sa, "broad ear", and Bara and Baragulla, probably "revealers" or "oracles". In addition, there was a daughter, Khi-dime-azaga, "child of the renowned spirit". She may have been identical to Belit-Sheri, who is referred to in the Sumerian hymns as the sister of Tammuz. This family group was probably formed by symbolizing the attributes of Ea and his spouse Damkina. Tammuz, in his character as a patriarch, may have been regarded as a hostage from the gods: the human form of Ea, who instructed mankind, like King Osiris, how to grow corn and cultivate fruit trees. As the youth who perished annually, he was the corn-spirit. He is referred to in the Bible by his Babylonian name.

When Ezekiel detailed the various idolatrous practices of the Israelites, which included the worship of the sun and "every form of creeping things and abominable beasts"--a suggestion of the composite monsters of Babylonia--he was brought "to the door of the gate of the Lord's house, which was towards the north; and, behold, there sat women weeping for Tammuz"

The weeping ceremony was connected with agricultural rites. Corn deities were weeping deities, they shed fertilizing tears, and the sowers simulated the sorrow of divine mourners when they cast seed in the soil "to die" so that it might spring up as corn. This ancient custom, like many others, contributed to the poetic imagery of the Bible. "They that sow in tears", David sang, "shall reap in joy. He that goeth forth and weepeth, bearing precious seed, shall doubtless come again with rejoicing, bringing his sheaves with him."In Egypt, the priestesses who acted the parts of Isis and Nephthys mourned for the slain corn god Osiris.

Gods and men before the face of the gods are weeping for
they at the same time, when they behold me!...
All thy sister goddesses are at thy side and behind thy couch,
Calling upon thee with weeping--yet thou are prostrate upon
thy bed!...
Live before us, wishing to behold thee.

It was believed to be essential that human beings should share the universal sorrow caused by the death of a god. If they remained unsympathetic, the deities would punish them as enemies. Worshippers of nature gods, therefore, based their ceremonial practices on natural phenomena. "The dread of the worshippers that the neglect of the usual ritual would be followed by disaster is particularly intelligible", writes Professor Robertson Smith, "if they regarded the necessary operations of agriculture as involving the violent extinction of a particle of divine life." By observing their ritual, the worshippers won the sympathy and cooperation of deities or exercised magical control over nature.

The Babylonian myth of Tammuz, the dying god, bears a close resemblance to the Greek myth of Adonis. It also links with the myth of Osiris. According to Professor Sayce, Tammuz is identical to "Daonus or Daos, the shepherd of Pantibibla", referred to by Berosus as the ruler of one of the mythical ages of Babylonia. We have therefore to deal with Tammuz in his twofold character as a patriarch and a god of fertility.

The Adonis version of the myth may be summarized. Ere the god was born, his mother, who was pursued by her angry sire, as the river goddesses of the folk tales are pursued by the good demons, transformed herself into a tree. Adonis sprang from the trunk of this tree, and Aphrodite, having placed the child in a chest, committed him to the care of Persephone, queen of Hades, who resembles the Babylonian Eresh-ki-gal. Persephone desired to retain the young god, and Aphrodite (Ishtar) appealed to Zeus (Anu), who decreed that Adonis should spend part of the year with one goddess and part of the year with the other.

It is suggested that the myth of Adonis was derived in post-Homeric times by the Greeks indirectly from Babylonia through the Western Semites, the Semitic title "Adon", meaning "lord", having been mistaken for a proper name. This theory, however, cannot be accepted without qualifications. It does not explain the existence of either the Phrygian myth of Attis, which was developed differently from the Tammuz myth or the Celtic story of "Diarmid and the boar", which belongs to the archaeological "Hunting Period". There are traces in Greek mythology of pre-Hellenic myths about dying harvest deities, like Hyakinthos and Erigone, for instance, who appear to have been mourned for. There is every possibility, therefore, that the Tammuz ritual may have been attached to a harvest god of the pre-Hellenic Greeks, who received at the same time the new name of Adonis. Osiris of Egypt resembles Tammuz, but his Mesopotamian origin has not been proved. It would appear probable that Tammuz, Attis, Osiris, and the deities represented by Adonis and Diarmid were all developed from an archaic god of fertility and vegetation, the central figure of a myth which was not only as ancient as the knowledge and practice of agriculture, but had existed even in the "Hunting Period". Traces of the Tammuz-Osiris story in various forms are found all over the area occupied by the Mediterranean or Brown race from Sumeria to the British Isles. The original myth was connected with tree and water worship and the worship of animals. Adonis sprang from a tree; the body of Osiris was concealed in a tree which grew round the sea-drifted chest in which he was concealed. Diarmid concealed himself in a tree when pursued by Finn. The blood of Tammuz, Osiris, and Adonis reddened the swollen rivers which fertilized the soil. Various animals were associated with the harvest god, who appears to have been manifested from time to time in different forms, for his spirit pervaded all nature. In Egypt, the soul of Osiris entered the Apis bull or the ram of Mendes.

Tammuz in the hymns is called "the pre-eminent steer of heaven", and a popular sacrifice was "a white kid of the god Tammuz", which, however, might be substituted by a sucking pig. Osiris had also associations with swine, and the Egyptians, according to Herodotus, sacrificed a pig to him annually. When Set at full moon hunted the boar in the Delta marshes, he probably hunted the boar form of Osiris, whose human body had been recovered from the sacred tree by Isis. As the soul of Bata, the hero of the Egyptian folk tale,

Tammuz in the hymns is called "the pre-eminent steer of heaven", and a popular sacrifice was "a white kid of the god Tammuz", which, however, might be substituted by a sucking pig. Osiris had also associations with swine, and the Egyptians, according to Herodotus, sacrificed a pig to him annually. When Set at full moon hunted the boar in the Delta marshes, he probably hunted the boar form of Osiris, whose human body had been recovered from the sacred tree by Isis. As the soul of Bata, the hero of the Egyptian folk tale migrated from the blossom to the bull, and the bull to the tree so apparently did the soul of Osiris pass from incarnation to incarnation. Set, the demon slayer of the harvest god had also a boar form; he was the black pig who devoured the waning moon and blinded the Eye of Ra.

migrated from the blossom to the bull, and the bull to the tree so apparently did the soul of Osiris pass from incarnation to incarnation. Set, the demon slayer of the harvest god had also a boar form; he was the black pig who devoured the waning moon and blinded the Eye of Ra.

Tammuz of the Sumerian hymns, however, is the Adonis-like god who lived on earth for a part of the year as the shepherd and agriculturist so dearly beloved by the goddess Ishtar. Then he died so that he might depart to the realm of Eresh-ki-gal (Persephone), queen of Hades. According to one account, his death was caused by the fickle Ishtar. When that goddess wooed Gilgamesh, the Babylonian Hercules, he upbraided her, saying:

On Tammuz, the spouse of thy youth,
Thou didst lay affliction every year.

References in the Sumerian hymns suggest that there also existed a form of the legend which gave an account of the slaying of the young god by someone else than Ishtar. The slayer may have been a Set-like demon--perhaps Nin-such, who appears to have symbolized the destroying influence of the sun. He was a war deity, and his name, Professor Pinches says, "is conjectured to mean 'lord of the wild boar'". There is no direct evidence, however, to connect Tammuz's slayer with the boar which killed Adonis. Ishtar's innocence is emphasized by the fact that she mourned for her youthful lover, crying:

Oh hero, my lord, ah me! I will say;
Food I eat not ... the water I drink not ...
Because of the exalted one of the nether world, him of the radiant face, yea radiant,
Of the exalted one of the nether world, him of the dove-like voice, yea dove-like.

The Phrygian Attis met his death, according to one legend, by self-mutilation under a sacred tree. Another account sets forth, however, that he was slain by a boar. The Greek Adonis was similarly killed by a boar. This animal was a form of Ares (Mars), god of war and tempest, who also loved Aphrodite (Ishtar). The Celtic Diarmid, in his character as a loving god, with lunar attributes, was slain by "the green boar", which appears to have been one of the animals of a ferocious Hag, an earth and air "mother" with various names. In one of the many Fingalian stories the animal is

... That venomous boar, and he so fierce,
That Gray eyebrow had with her herd of swine.

Diarmid had eloped with the wife of Finn-mac-Coul (Fingal), who, like Ares, plotted to bring about his rival's death, and accordingly set the young hero to hunt the boar. As a thunder god, Finn carried a hammer with which he smote his shield; the blows were heard in Lochlann (Scandinavia). Diarmid, like Tammuz, the "god of the tender voice and shining eyes", had much beauty. When he expired, Finn cried:

No maiden will raise her eye
Since the mold has gone over thy visage fair...
Blue without rashness in the thin eyes!
Passion and beauty behind thy curls!...
Oh, yesternight it was green the hillock,
Red is it this day with Diarmid's blood.

Tammuz died with the dying vegetation, and Diarmid expired when the hills were assuming their purple tints. The month of Tammuz wailings was from 20th June till 20th July, when the heat and dryness brought forth the demons of pestilence. The mourners chanted:

He has gone, he has gone to the bosom of the earth,
And the dead are numerous in the land...
Men are filled with sorrow: they stagger by day in the gloom ...
In the month of thy year which brings not peace hast thou gone.
Thou hast gone on a journey that makes an end of thy people.

The following extract contains a reference to the slaying of the god:

The holy one of Ishtar, in the middle of the year the fields
languish...
The shepherd, the wise one, the man of sorrows, why they have
slain?...
In his temple, in his inhabited domain,
The child, lord of knowledge, abides no more...
In the meadows, verily, the soul of life perishes.

There is wailing for Tammuz "at the sacred cedar, where the mother bore thee", a reference which connects the god, like Adonis and Osiris, with tree worship:

The wailing is for the herbs: the first lament is, "they are not
produced".
The wailing is for the grain, ears are not produced.
The wailing is for the habitations, for the flocks which bring forth no more.

The wailing is for the perishing wedded ones; for the perishing
children; the dark-headed people create no more.

The wailing is also for the shrunken river, the parched meadows, the fishpools, the cane brakes, the forests, the plains, the gardens, and the palace, which all suffer because the god of fertility has departed. The mourner cries:

How long shall the springing of verdure be restrained?
How long shall the putting forth of leaves be held back?

Whither went Tammuz? His destination has already been referred to as "the bosom of the earth", and in the Assyrian version of the "Descent of Ishtar" he dwells in "the house of darkness" among the dead, "where dust is their nourishment and their food mud", and "the light is never seen"--the gloomy Babylonian Hades. In one of the Sumerian hymns, however, it is stated that Tammuz "upon the flood was cast out". The reference may be to the submarine "house of Ea", or the Blessed Island to which the Babylonian Noah was carried. In this Hades bloomed the nether "garden of Adonis".

The following extract refers to the garden of Damu (Tammuz):--

Damu his youth therein slumbers ...
Among the garden flowers he slumbers; among the garden flowers
he is cast away ...
Among the tamarisks he slumbers, with woe he causes us to be
satiated.

Although Tammuz of the hymns was slain, he returned from Hades. He came back as a child. He is wailed for as "child, Lord Gishzida", as well as "my hero Damu". In his lunar character, the Egyptian Osiris appeared each month as "the child surpassingly beautiful"; the Osiris bull was also a child of the moon; "it was begotten", says Plutarch, "by a ray of generative light falling from the moon". When the bull of Attis was sacrificed his worshippers were drenched with its blood and were afterward ceremonially fed with milk, as they were supposed to have "renewed their youth" and become children. The ancient Greek god Eros (Cupid) was represented as a wanton boy or handsome youth. Another god of fertility, the Irish Angus, who resembles Eros, is called "the ever young"; he slumbers like Tammuz and awakes in the Spring.

It was thought that, like Vyasa and other Indian mythological super-men, Tammuz, a child god, had returned from the previous Sumerian Paradise of the Deep and had quickly reached adulthood. A terse couplet from a Tammuz hymn reads:

He was a baby when the boat he was in went down.
In the hidden grain, he lay in his manhood.

The "boat" may be the "chest" in which Adonis was concealed by Aphrodite when she confided him to the care of Persephone, queen of Hades, who desired to retain the young god but was compelled by Zeus to send him back to the goddess of love and vegetation. The fact that Ishtar descended to Hades in quest of Tammuz may perhaps explain the symbolic references in hymns to mother goddesses being in sunken boats also when their powers were in abeyance, as were those of the god for part of each year. It is possible, too, that the boat had a lunar and a solar significance. Khonsu, the Egyptian moon god, for instance, was associated with the Spring sun, being a deity of fertility and therefore a corn spirit; he was a form of Osiris, the Patriarch, who sojourned on earth to teach mankind how to grow corn and cultivate fruit trees. In the Egyptian legend

Osiris received the corn seeds from Isis, which suggests that among Great-Mother-worshipping peoples, it was believed that agricultural civilization had a female origin. The same myths may have been attached to corn gods and corn goddesses, associated with water, sun, moon, and stars.

That there existed in Babylonia at an extremely remote period an agricultural myth regarding a Patriarch of divine origin who was rescued from a boat in his childhood, is suggested by the legend which was attached to the memory of the usurper King Sargon of Akkad. It runs as follows:

"Sargon, the powerful King of Akkad, is who I am. My father was an alien whose brother lived on the mountain, and my mother was a vestal (priestess). My mother gave birth to me at a secret location after my conception. She put me in a rush-lined container, sealed the door with pitch, and threw me into the river.

The river carried me to Akki, the water drawer, who pulled me forward while drawing water. As his son and gardener, Akki, the water drawer, schooled me. Ishtar, the goddess of gardens, loved me." "

It is unlikely that this story was invented by Sargon. Like the many variants of it found in other countries, it was probably founded on a form of the Tammuz-Adonis myth. Indeed, a new myth would not have suited Sargon's purpose so well as the adaptation of an old one, which was more likely to make a popular appeal when connected with his name. The references to the goddess Ishtar, and Sargon's early life as a gardener, suggest that the king desired to be remembered as an agricultural Patriarch, if not of the divine, at any rate of semi-divine origin.

What appears to be an early form of the widespread Tammuz myth is the Teutonic legend regarding the mysterious child who came over the sea to inaugurate a new era of civilization and instruct the people on how to grow corn and become great warriors. The Northern peoples, as archaeological evidence suggests, derived their knowledge of agriculture, and therefore their agricultural myths, from the Neolithic representatives of the Mediterranean race with whom they came into contact. There can be no doubt that the Teutonic legend refers to the introduction of agriculture. The child is called "Stef" or "Scarf", which signifies "Sheaf", or "Scyld, the son of Scarf". Scyld is the patriarch of the Scyldings, the Danes, a people of mixed origin. In the Anglo-Saxon _Beowulf_ poem, the reference is to "Scyld", but Ethelweard, William of Malmesbury, and others adhered to "Scarf" as the name of the Patriarch of the Western Saxons.

The legend runs that one day a boat was seen approaching the shore; it was not propelled by oars or sail. In it lay a child fast asleep, his head pillowed upon a sheaf of grain. He was surrounded by armor, treasure, and various implements, including the fire-borer. The child was reared by the people who found him, and he became a great instructor and warrior and ruled over the tribe as king. In _Beowulf_ Scyld is the father of the elder Beowulf, whose grandson Hrothgar built the famous Hall. The poem opens with a reference to the patriarch "Scyld of the Sheaf". When he died, his body, according to the request he had made, was laid in a ship that was set adrift:

Many riches that were going to enter the force of the river were laid out on his breast. He was given no fewer gifts or trinkets by them (the mourners) than by those who had first sent him across the sea by himself when he was a young child. They also placed a standard with gold embroidery high above his head beside him before allowing the torrent to carry him into the sea. They had a dejected attitude and a dejected soul. Men, chiefs of the council, and heroes beneath heaven cannot say with certainty who received that load.

Scarf or Scyld has characteristics with Yngve, the ancestor of the Ynglings, Frey, the harvest and boar god, and the following Hermod, who is mentioned in the Eddic "Lay of Hyndla":

He bestows wealth on some, war fame on his progeny, and
many people have good word skills, and men know,
Fair breezes to mariners, skaldic songcraft,
and many a fighter the power of manhood.

Tammuz is also known as "the sovereign, lord of invocation," "the wise one," "the ruler of knowledge," and "the heroic king of the country."

Heimdal, the watchman of the Teutonic gods, also dwelt for a time among men as "Rig", and had human offspring, his son Thrall being the ancestor of the Thralls, his son Churl of churls, and Jarl of noblemen.

Tammuz, like Heimdal, is also a guardian. He watches the flocks and herds, whom he guards against the Gallu demons as Heimdal guards the world and the heavens against attacks by giants and monsters. The flocks of Tammuz, Professor Pinches suggests, "recall the flocks of the Greek sun god Helios. These were the clouds illuminated by the sun, which were likened to sheep--indeed, one of the early Sumerian expressions for 'fleece' was 'sheep of the sky. The name of Tammuz in Sumerian is Dumu-zi, or in its rare fullest form, Dumuzida, meaning 'true or faithful son'. There is probably some legend attached to this which is at present unknown."

Therefore, the Sumerian hymn-singers bemoaned:

He (Tammuz) has abandoned the sheep and cattle sentinels like a herdsman.
The wise son and the top steer of heaven left his home and his inhabited territory and made his way to the underworld's herding grounds.

Agni, an Aryo-Indian god who shares characteristics with Heimdal as the sky sentinel, also shares similarities with Tammuz, particularly in his Mitra persona:

The son of the seas, Agni, has become well-known among the male tribal groups. Mitra is acting morally. Rigveda iii, 5 and 3

Agni, who has been looked and longed for in Heaven, who has been looked for on earth--he who has been looked for has entered all herbs. _Rigveda_, I, 98.

Tammuz, like the Egyptian lunar and solar god Khonsu, is "the healer", and Agni "drives away all disease". Tammuz is the god "of sonorous voice"; Agni "roars like a bull", and Heimdal blows a horn when the giants and demons threaten to attack the citadel of the gods. As the spring sun god, Tammuz is "a youthful warrior", says Jastrow, "triumphing over the storms of winter". The storms, of course, were symbolized by demons. Tammuz, "the heroic lord", was, therefore, a demon slayer like Heimdal and Agni. Each of these gods appears to have been developed in isolation from an archaic spring god of fertility and corn whose attributes were symbolized. In Teutonic mythology, for instance, Heimdal was the warrior form of the patriarch Scef, while Frey was the deified agriculturist who came over the deep as a child. In Saxo's mythical history of Denmark, Frey as Frode is taken prisoner by a storm giant, Beli, "the howler", and is loved by his hag sister in the Teutonic Hades, as Tammuz is loved by Eresh-ki-gal, spouse of the storm god Nergal, in the Babylonian Hades. Frode returns to earth, like

Tammuz, in due season.

There were various versions of the Tammuz myth in Ancient Babylonia. In one the goddess Ishtar visited Hades to search for the lover of her youth. A part of this form of the legend survives in the famous Assyrian hymn known as "The Descent of Ishtar ". It was first translated by the late Mr. George Smith, of the British Museum. A box containing inscribed tablets had been sent from Assyria to London, and Mr. Smith, with characteristic patience and skill, arranged and deciphered them, giving to the world a fragment of ancient literature infused with much sublimity and imaginative power. Ishtar is depicted descending to dismal Hades, where the souls of the dead exist in bird forms:

I spread like a bird my hands.
I descend, I descend to the house of darkness, the dwelling of the
god Irkalla:
To the house out of which there is no exit,
To the road from which there is no return:
To the house from whose entrance the light is taken,
The place where dust is their nourishment and their food mud.
Its chiefs are also like birds covered with feathers;
The light is never seen, in the darkness, they dwell...
Over the door and bolts is scattered dust.

When the goddess reaches the gate of Hades she cries to the porter:

Keeper of the waters, open thy gate,
Open thy gate that I may enter.
If thou openest not the gate that I may enter
I will strike the door, the bolts I will shatter,
I will strike the threshold and will pass through the doors;
I will raise the dead to devour the living,

Above the living, the dead shall exceed in numbers.

The porter replies that he must first speak with the Queen of Hades, who is identified as Allahu here. He then informs Allahu about the Queen of Heaven's arrival. Allahu refers to individuals who Ishtar ordered to perish while expressing his wrath:

Let me cry for the strong who have abandoned their wives, for the handmaidens who have lost their husbands' hugs.

Let me weep for my one and only kid, who was snatched from me before his time.

Then she suddenly offers the severe order:

Go, keeper, let her through the gate.

Bewitch her by the venerable laws;

i.e. "Handle her as you would the others that come here."

As Ishtar enters through the various gates she is stripped of her ornaments and clothing. At the first gate, her crown was taken off, at the second her ear-rings, at the third her necklace of precious stones, at the fourth the ornaments of her breast, at the fifth, she gemmed waist-girdle, at the sixth the bracelets of her hands and feet, and at the seventh the covering robe of her body. Ishtar asks at each gate why she is thus dealt with, and the porter answers, "Such is the command of Allahu."

After descending for a prolonged period the Queen of Heaven at length stands naked before the Queen of Hades. Ishtar is proud and arrogant, and Allahu, desiring to punish her rival whom she cannot humble,

requests that the plague demon Namtar smite her with sickness throughout

various bodily components. Ishtar's demise had a terrible impact on

Earth: Fertility and growth were no longer possible.

The gods' messenger, Pap-sukal, meantime, hurried to Shamash, the solar god to explain what had happened. The sun god at once consulted the deep god Ea and his moon father Sin. and then created Nadushu-Namir, a man-lion, to save Ishtar, giving him the ability to enter Hades' seven gates. before this being transmitted his message

Allahu ... struck her breast; she bit her thumb,
She turned again: a request she asked not.

In her anger, she cursed the rescuer of the Queen of Heaven.

May I imprison thee in the great prison,
May the garbage of the foundations of the city be thy food,
May the drains of the city be thy drink,
May the darkness of the dungeon be thy dwelling,
May the stake be thy seat,
May hunger and thirst strike thy offspring.

She was compelled, however, to obey the high gods, and addressed Namtar, saying:

Unto Ishtar give the waters of life and bring her before me.

Thereafter the Queen of Heaven was conducted through the various gates, and at each, she received her robe and the ornaments which were taken from her on entering. Namtar says:

Since thou hast not paid a ransom for thy deliverance to her (Allahu), so to her again turn back, For Tammuz the husband of thy youth. The glistening waters (of life) pour over him... In splendid clothing dress him, with a ring of crystal adorn him.

Ishtar mourns for "the wound of Tammuz", smiting her breast, and she did not ask for "the precious eye-stones, her amulets", which were apparently to ransom Tammuz. The poem concludes with Ishtar's wail:

You don't grieve for me, Tammuz, my lone brother.
On the day of Tammuz, he adorned me with a crystal ring, an emerald bracelet, and himself. [123] May men mourners and women mourners.
Place him on a bier and gather everyone for the wake.

An ancient Sumerian hymn to Tammuz sheds some light on this story. It is stated that Tammuz either refused to return or was unable to do so when Ishtar begged him to be happy and take care of his flocks from Hades.

He sent his wife back to her home.

She then started the rite for weeping:

The seductive Queen of Heaven is united in the shadows.

The hymn Tammuz III, which Mr. Langdon also translates, appears to contain the story that served as the basis for the Assyrian translation. However, Belit-Sheri, not Ishtar, is the goddess who descended to Hades. The "gallu-demon," the "slayer," and other demons are with her when she converses with Tammuz, but their communication is "unintelligible and damaged." He reportedly commits to come back to Earth, though.

I'll ascend, and as for me, I'll leave with you.

I'll go back, so let's return to my mum.

Probably two goddesses originally lamented for Tammuz, as the Egyptian sisters, Isis and Nephthys, lamented for Osiris, their brother. Ishtar is referred to as "my mother". Isis figures alternately in the Egyptian chants as a mother, wife, sister, and daughter of Osiris. She cries, "Come thou to thy wife in peace; her heart fluttereth for thy love", ... "I am thy wife, made as thou art, the elder sister, soul of her brother".... "Come thou to us as a babe".... "Lo, thou art as the Bull of the two goddesses--come thou, a child growing in peace, our lord!"... "Lo! the Bull, begotten of the two cows, Isis and Nephthys".... "Come thou to the two widowed goddesses"... "Oh child, lord, the first maker of the body".... "Father Osiris."

Isis and Nephthys cry for Osiris in the same way that Ishtar and Belit-Sheri do for Tammuz.

I'm calling out to you while sobbing, but you're lying on your bed!
When they see me, both gods and humans "are grieving for thee at the same moment" (Isis).
Lo! I call to you in a voice as high as the heavens.

Isis and Hathor (Ishtar), the cow, are also related. The cow can be heard crying out for you.

There is another phase, however, to the character of the mother goddess which explains the references to the desertion and slaying of Tammuz by Ishtar. "She is", says Jastrow, "the goddess of the human instinct, or passion which accompanies human love. Gilgamesh ... reproaches her with abandoning the objects of her passion after a brief period of the union." At Ishtar's temple "public maidens accepted temporary partners, assigned to them by Ishtar".[128] The worship of all mother goddesses in ancient times was accompanied by revolting unmoral rites which are referred to in condemnatory terms in various passages in the Old Testament, especially in connection with the worship of Ashtoreth, who was identical to Ishtar and the Egyptian Hathor.

Ishtar in the process of time overshadowed all the other female deities of Babylonia, as did Isis in Egypt. Her name, indeed, which is Semitic, became in the plural, Ishtaráte, a designation for goddesses in general. But although she was referred to as the daughter of the sky, Anu, or the daughter of the moon, Sin or Nannar, she still retained traces of her ancient character. Originally she was a great mother goddess, who was worshipped by those who believed that life and the universe had a female origin in contrast to those who believed in the theory of male origin. Ishtar is identical to Nina, the fish goddess, a creature who gave her name to the Sumerian city of Nina and the Assyrian city of Nineveh. Other forms of the Creatrix included Mama, or Mami, or Ama, "mother", Aruru, Bau, Gula, and Zerpanitu^{m}. These were all "Preservers" and healers. At the same time, they were "Destroyers", like Nin-sun and the Queen of Hades, Eresh-ki-gal, or Allahu. They were accompanied by shadowy male forms ere they became wives of strongly individualized gods, or by child gods, their sons, who might be regarded as "brothers" or "husbands of their mothers", to use the paradoxical Egyptian term. Similarly, Great Father deities had vaguely defined wives. The "Semitic" Baal, "the lord", was accompanied by a female reflection of himself-- Belt, "the lady". Shamash, the sun god, had for his wife the shadowy Aa.

As has been shown, Ishtar is referred to in a Tammuz hymn as the mother of the child god of fertility. In an Egyptian hymn the sky goddess Nut, "the mother" of Osiris, is stated to have "built up life from her own body". Sri or Lakshmi, the Indian goddess, who became the wife of Vishnu, as the mother goddess Saraswati, a tribal deity, became the wife of Brahma, was, according to a Purana commentator, "the mother of the world ... eternal and undecaying".

The gods, on the other hand, might die annually: the goddesses alone were immortal. Indra was supposed to perish of old age, but his wife, Indrani, remained ever young. There were fourteen Indras in every "day of Brahma", a reference apparently to the ancient conception of Indra among the Great-Mother-worshipping sections of the Aryo-Indians. In the _Mahabharata_ the god Shiva, as Mahadeva, commands Indra on "one of the peaks of Himavat", where they met, to lift a stone and join the Indras who had been before him. "And Indra on removing that stone beheld a cave on the breast of that king of mountains in which were four others resembling himself." Indra exclaimed in his grief, "Shall I be even like these?" These five Indras, like the "Seven Sleepers", awaited the time when they would be called forth. They were ultimately reborn as the five Pandavas warriors.

The ferocious, black-faced Scottish mother goddess, Cailleach Bheur, who appears to be identical to Mala Lith, "Grey Eyebrows" of Fingalian story, and the English "Black Annis", figures in Irish song and legend as "The Old Woman of Beare". This "old woman" (Cailleach) "had", says Professor Kuno Meyer, "seven periods of youth one after another, so that every man who had lived with her came to die of old age, and her grandsons and great-grandsons were tribes and races". When old age at length came upon her she sang her "swan song", from which the following lines are extracted:

To me, the ebb tide is like the sea.
My old age is an embarrassment.
It is wealthy.
Love, it's not the men.
When we were alive, we had a thing for guys.
When they are not covered, my arms are skeletal and thin;
when they are, they were once round, gorgeous rulers.
I must put on clothing in the sunlight because my renewal time is near.

The Germanic mother goddess Freyja, whose cat-drawn carriage had a large number of lovers. Loki mocks her in the Icelandic poem "Lokasenna," saying:

Keep quiet, Freyja! I am well aware of the fact that you are immaculate; each god and elf present here has been chosen by you as a partner.

Similar language is used to address Idun, the keeper of the apples of perpetual youth that stop the gods from aging:

Idun, be silent! Who couldst throw those fair-washed arms of thine Around thy brother's murderer? I swear, of all ladies, you are the most wanton.

Odin's wife Frigg is also made fun of:

Frigg, keep quiet! You are the wife of the Earth and have always desired for men!

The goddesses of classic mythology had similar reputations. Aphrodite (Venus) had many divine and mortal lovers. She links closely with Astarte and Ashtoreth (Ishtar), and reference has already been made to her relations with Adonis (Tammuz). These love deities were all as cruel as they were wayward. When Ishtar wooed the Babylonian hero, Gilgamesh, he spurned her advances, as has been indicated, saying:

On Tammuz, the spouse of thy youth,
Thou didst lay affliction every year.
Thou didst love the brilliant Allahu bird
But thou didst smite him and break his wing;
He stands in the woods and cries "O my wing".

He likewise charged her with deceiving the lion and the horse, making reference to obscure myths:

Thou didst also love a shepherd of the flock,
Who continually poured out for the libation,
And daily slaughtered kids for thee;
But thou didst smite him and didst change him into a

leopard,
So that his sheep boy hunted him,
And his hounds tore him to pieces.

These goddesses were always willing to harm those who might offend them or who they grew weary of. Ascalaphus was transformed into an owl by Demeter (Ceres), while Stellio became a lizard. Ops Rhea resembled

Mother of one hundred gods and the towered Cybele

the wanton who loved Attis (Adonis). Artemis (Diana) slew her lover Orion, changed Actaeon into a stag, which was torn to pieces by his dogs, and caused numerous deaths by sending a boar to ravage the fields of Oeneus, king of Calydon. Human sacrifices were frequently offered to the bloodthirsty "mothers". The most famous victim of Artemis was the daughter of Agamemnon, "divinely tall and most divinely fair". Agamemnon had slain a sacred stag, and the goddess punished him by sending a calm when the war fleet was about to sail for Troy, with the result that his daughter had to be sacrificed. Artemis thus sold breezes like the northern wind hags and witches.

It used to be customary to account for the similarities manifested by the various mother goddesses by assuming that there was constant cultural contact between separate nationalities, and, as a result, a not inconsiderable amount of "religious borrowing". Greece was supposed to have received its great goddesses from the western Semites, who had come under the spell of Babylonian religion. Archaeological evidence, however, tends to disprove this theory. "The most recent researches into Mesopotamian history", writes Dr. Farnell, "establish with certainty the conclusion that there was no direct political contact possible between the powers in the valley of the Euphrates and the western shores of the Aegean in the second millennium B.C. In fact, between the nascent Hellas and the great world of Mesopotamia, there were powerful and possibly independent strata of cultures interposing."

The real connection appears to be the racial one. Among the Mediterranean Neolithic tribes of Sumeria, Arabia, and Europe, the goddess cult appears to have been influential. Mother worship was the predominant characteristic of their religious systems so the Greek goddesses were probably of pre-Hellenic origin, the Celtic of Iberian, the Egyptian of proto-Egyptian, and the Babylonian of Sumerian. The northern hillmen, on the other hand, who may be identified with the "Aryans" of the philologists, were father worshippers. The Vedic Aryo-Indians worshipped father gods,[138] as did also the Germanic peoples and certain tribes in the "Hittite confederacy". Earth spirits were males, like the Teutonic elves, the Aryo-Indian Ribhus, and the Burkans, "masters", of the present-day Buriats, a Mongolian people. When the father-worshipping peoples invaded the dominions of the mother-worshipping peoples, they introduced their strongly individualized gods, but they did not displace the mother goddesses. "The Aryan Hellenes", says Dr. Farnell, "were able to plant their Zeus and Poseidon on the high hill of Athens, but not to overthrow the supremacy of Athena in the central shrine and the aboriginal soul of the Athenian people." As in Egypt, the beliefs of the father worshippers, represented by the self-created Ptah, were fused with the beliefs of the mother worshippers, who adored Isis, Mut, Neith, and others. In Babylonia, this process of racial and religious fusion was well advanced before the dawn of history. Ea, who had already assumed manifold forms, may have originally been the son or child lover of Damkina, "Lady of the Deep", as was Tammuz of Ishtar. As the fish, Ea was the offspring of the mother river.

The mother worshippers recognized the male as well as female deities but regarded the great goddess as the First Cause. Although the primeval spirits were grouped in four pairs in Egypt, and apparently in Babylonia also, the female in the first pair was more strongly individualized than the male. The Egyptian Nu is vaguer than his consort Nut, and the Babylonian Apsu than his consort Tiamat. Indeed, in the narrative of the Creation Tablets of Babylon, which will receive full treatment in a later chapter, Tiamat, the great mother, is the controlling spirit. She is more powerful and ferocious than Apsu and lives longer. After Apsu's death, she elevates one of her brood, named Kingu, to be her consort, a fact which suggests that the Ishtar-Tammuz myth survives the influence of exceedingly ancient modes of thought. Like Tiamat, Ishtar is also a great battle heroine, and in this capacity, she was addressed as "the lady of majestic rank exalted over all gods". This was no idle flattery on the part of worshippers, but a memory of her ancient supremacy.

Reference has been made to the introduction of Tammuz worship into Jerusalem. Ishtar, as Queen of Heaven, was also adored by the backsliding Israelites as a deity of battle and harvest. When Jeremiah censured the people for burning incense and serving gods "whom they knew not", he said, "neither they, ye, nor your fathers", they made answered: "Since we left off to burn incense to the queen of heaven, and to pour out drink offerings unto her, we have wanted all things, and have been consumed by the sword and the famine". The women took a leading part in these practices but refused to accept all the blame, saying, "When we burned incense to the queen of heaven and poured out drink offerings unto her, did we make our cakes and pour out drink offerings unto her without our men?" That the husbands, and the children even, assisted at the ceremony is made evident in another reference to goddess worship: "The children gather wood, and the fathers kindle the fire, and the women knead the dough, to make cakes to the queen of heaven"

Jastrow suggests that the women of Israel wept for Tammuz, and offered cakes to the mother goddess, &c., because "in all religious bodies ... women represent the conservative element; among them, religious customs continue in practice after they have been abandoned by men".[142] The evidence of Jeremiah, however, shows that the men certainly co-operated at the archaic ceremonials. In lighting the fires with the "vital spark", they acted in imitation of the god of fertility. The women, on the other hand, represented the reproductive harvest goddess in providing the food supply. In recognition of her gift, they rewarded the goddess by offering her the cakes prepared from the new ground wheat and barley--the "first fruits of the harvest". As the corn god came as a child, the children began the ceremony by gathering the wood for the sacred fire. When the women mourned for Tammuz, they did so evidently because the death of the god was lamented by the goddess Ishtar. It would appear, therefore, that the suggestion regarding the "conservative element" should apply to the immemorial practices of folk religion. These differed from the refined ceremonies of the official cult in Babylonia, where there were suitable temples and organized bands of priests and priestesses. But the official cult received no recognition in Palestine; the cakes intended for a goddess were not offered up in the temple of Abraham's God, but "in the streets of Jerusalem" and those of other cities.

The logical conclusion would seem to be that in ancient times, women played a significant role in ceremonial folk worship of the Great Mother goddess everywhere, while males participated in the smaller role of the god she had created and later received as "husband of his mother." This may explain why women have a high social status among goddess worshippers, such as those of the Mediterranean race, whose early religion was tightly entwined with daily activities rather than being restricted to temples.

9 798887 830766